Jottings from Jean Way

Cut courtesy of Southwestern Engraving Co.

Jean Way

What do little girls talk about?
What is their mystic theme?
Those still too young for puppy love,
Yet old enough to dream.

— William Herschell

Jottings from Jean Way

Library of Congress Catalog Card No. 79-185838

Printed in the United States of America

ISBN 0-8111-0447-8

Foreword

Was it Goethe who said, "Talent alone cannot make the writer, there must be a man behind the book?" In this day of Women's Lib, it can be a woman. Behind this book is Jean Way.

Jean and I met on the campus of The University of Texas and later taught together here in San Antonio. Then, one summer Jean decided to go to Europe and for one reason or another failed to get back to San Antonio for thirty-five years. Our friendship during this time was held together by an occasional note and the usual Christmas cards. One day a torn page from the 1924 Brackenridge annual arrived. It was the dedication page with our pictures. On the margin was written, "I am returning to San Antonio" — no other message.

That was eleven years ago. The thirty-five year gap disappeared. It was 1924 again. She was the same gay, stimulating person I had known then: one with whom you enjoyed touring the West on a Greyhound Bus, treking through Europe, spending an evening discussing a book or play, reviewing the happenings of the day or having her read a poem she had just composed while washing the dishes.

These verses represent subjects that have caught her fancy, or that reflect a mood. They have delighted the recipients, for each was written with a particular person in mind.

Is she to be judged a poet or a rhymster? "Common sense of readers uncorrupted with literary prejudice must finally decide all claims to potential honours."

– Ximena Wolf

Preface

When I should be heeding the news
I spend my time courting the muse.

Contents

Introduction

One of the bright little recollections I have of Jean Way as my journalism teacher in the early days of Brackenridge High School is of her urging everyone in the class to learn at least one new word every day. "Take the word 'ubiquitous,'" she said as she removed a hairpin from her hair, held it up and added: "The ubiquitous hairpin. You find it everywhere." She then hastened to declare that no one actually would so dignify a hairpin. But ubiquitous is a word I never forgot. Jean Way has always known how to use words most skillfully and what could be more to the point than the delightful contents of this little book.

– Renwicke Cary

Trivia

Oral Dialogue

(Lady patient with inflamed gums)

J.W. vs. J.L.

J.W.: I may be allergic
To stuff metallurgic
So I'm back.

J.L.: It's placque.

J.W.: Please look and see.
Of vitamin B
I may have a lack.

J.L.: It's placque.

J.W.: On closer inspection –
A major infection?
Or minor attack?

J.L.: I say it's placque –
Placque – plaque –
Placque!

To J. L. Larkin
A high mark in
Ignoring the "clacque"
And sticking to placque.

(Censored)

By all literary criteria
This is unadulterated trivia.
No reviews in national media –
Let's consign it to "oblivia."

This may hurt the author's vanity,
But we'll surely save our sanity
And curtail Jean Way's profanity:
Not "damn it to hell" – only "damity."

To Jo

Lover of cats and dogs
But not of turtles and frogs

Ho! Ho!

To a needy benefactress
When they're in some mess

So-So

From her aging leading lady
Name of Jean (she's not Sadie*)

HAPPY BIRTHDAY

* Sadie Thompson

Tale End?

(In answer to a letter from Mr. Lester Hamilton stating that he would be here at the "tale end of the week.")

Was "tale" a pun
And just for fun?
    (See last letter to this lady.*)
Can "tale" mean end?
If so my friend,
    you could be here by Friday.

* Cockney pronunciation

To Lester Hamilton

Alas and alack a-day
The shoemaker's children, they say,
    Have no shoes on their feet
    As they pad up the street
Though Dad sits a-cobbling all day.

A typo's not good – it's real bad
In a job for ourselves I might add.
    But working for you
    We catch them, we do!
We're all mighty proud of Gol-yad!

Hail the Chief!*

See page 2, Homecoming Edition, *Independent Star-News*: "Author of . . . 'Voices of the Airways' . . . and a prolific writer of verse published elsewhere."

Don't you want ANY bookstores to know where to buy your books?

Yours (As before!)

*Letter to a Naylor Company author and carbons of the three-page reply went to:

Mrs. Joe O. Naylor

Mrs. Retting

Mr. Julian Dickenson

Mr. John Smith

For Jean and Earl

Four blissful years
Mostly smiles — a few tears,
So few you can't remember.

To help you mark the day
This greeting from Jean Way
On the ninth day of September.

1971

Hark, the Mews (Muse)
A Collection of Cat Doggerel

Scat?

Hunger in the city –
    I ignore unpleasant news.
But hunger on my doorstep,
    Expressed in Maltese mews,
Awakened tender pity
    For a starving mama cat
And four hungry nursing kittens –
I could not tell them, "Scat!"

Mews in Maltese

Oh kittens, deah
Come heah – come heah!
    Somebody's heard my mews.

Here's food galoah
We eat once moah
    Indeed, this is good news!

My Four Little Kittens

My four little kittens
    Don't have no mittens
That's why they've begun to cry,
    "Oh mama dear, see here, see here
        Our feet are cold and bare,
    So cold and bare, oh where, oh where,
        Are mittens to be found?"
My po' little kittens
    Without no mittens
Between footsies and cold ground.

Why Not, for Kitty's Sake?

Mama cat is very sad;
    No one has named her kittens
Puss-in-Boots is not too bad
    For blackie who has four white mittens.

For blackie with a collar white
    Padre is a name most fittin'
But then it wouldn't be quite right
    If he should be a female kitten.

Batman should do very well,
    But doubts arise as this is written.
Can it be good? Oh what the hell!
    It's plenty good for a coal black kitten.

Now for the last, the Maltese gray
    I sit and think and keep a-sittin'.
Male? Or female? Oh, either way —
    The Wee Gray Nun I'll call this kitten.

Kitten-Nippers

Puss-in-Boots and Padre cat
    Are just like any other kittens –
Black with white, and soft and fat –
    They leave me quite unsmitten.

The Wee Gray Nun is timid, shy –
    A winsome, wobbly, bewitching kitten.
A convent kitten would this imply?
    Very likely, her sex permittin'.

Coal black Batman, bold as brass,
    A hissing, spitting, fearless kitten,
A stalker in the alley grass –
    He's my favorite I am admittin'.

Where?

Where, oh where have my kitty cats gone?
    Where, oh where can they be?
I loved each kitten and now, doggone,
    They've up and deserted me.

Quiet as little mice they left
    (If *they*'ll pardon such an expression)
They've left me flat and sore bereft
    Sunk deep in dark depression.

Dear Whitey,

Connecticut cats go in for fashion
Pussy's gown is cool mint green
But pussy's heart is hot with passion
A feline vampire, a purring queen!

Greetings from the Poet Laureate of Catdom to your two human housekeepers and catnip suppliers.

To: *The Right Honorable Whitey Cat, Esq.*
Lord of Catnip Alley
Chief Caterwauler of Sunshine Drive

Felis Penitentis

I climbed the fence at midnight,
    Meowing my mating song.
I walked the fence in the moonlight.
    Tell me, was that wrong?

I was dressed in the latest fashion –
    My gown was slinky and long.
My heart was hot with passion –
    Tell me, was that wrong?

Only a cop, a filthy louse,
    Heeded my siren song.
He carted me off to the station house –
    Tell me, wasn't that wrong?

So, here I am, dear Whitey Cat,
    Singing a penitent song.
I promise I'll never do this or that
    I'll never again go wrong!

The Author

Jean Way—*the* Jean Way—is an unforgettable individual. Singularity of character, indomitability of spirit, or any number of other terms could be used in a description, but none would really capture her personality.

Some people, on first acquaintance, are cowed. Some are impressed; some are offended; some are delighted. None are indifferent. An awareness of self and an irreproachable sense of dignity are characteristic. A fascinating, dramatic and unending dialog compels further investigation.

So does her writing. Whether industriously creating a dust jacket or jotting off whimsical lines to a captivated author, Miss Way has a facility for words which is unmatched. Beginning with vocabulary games around the family dining table in Alpine, Texas, and encouraged by both mother and father, she has always striven for precision of expression. That unique flair has been the basis of a long and impressive career.

Her four sisters and her lifelong friends watched

with both pride and fear as she set off alone to New York to establish a career rather than find the easiest or most obvious job at home. Miss Way has never compromised with mediocrity. She has, therefore, always succeeded in achieving excellence.

Graduating Phi Beta Kappa in English from The University of Texas, for forty years she influenced people's taste in everything from linens to retail dresses. She served as editor of a fashion magazine, did advertising and publicity for Fifth Avenue department stores including Altman's, and was responsible for national publicity exclusively for ten years with three important New York advertising agencies, including Amos Parrish, handling product publicity and two industry accounts.

She was account executive for the Irish Linen Industry – including advertising, publicity, promotion, and a sales training program. Her news releases have been published under the by-line of the women's page editor in metropolitan newspapers from New England to California. She has written industrial movie scripts and supervised the photography for the Irish Linen Industry, for U. S. Rubber and for various free-lance assignments.

Never-to-be-forgotten, always-to-be-loved, Miss Way now makes her home at The Naylor Company in San Antonio.